How Do Plants Grow Here?

Written by Anna Porter

Series Consultant: Linda Hoyt

WorldWise™
Content-based Learning

Contents

Introduction

Some plants can grow in **harsh** places where most other plants would die. These can be hot, dry, rocky places, very cold places or salty water.

How do these plants get what they need to survive in these places?

Chapter 1

How do plants grow in hot, dry places?

Some plants can grow in hot, dry places and still get the water they need.

Growing in hot, dry deserts

Some desert plants have tiny hairs on their leaves, and these hairs trap rainwater for the plants to use. The seeds from these plants are blown to other parts of the desert. When it rains again, these seeds grow very quickly into new plants.

Cacti grow in the desert.

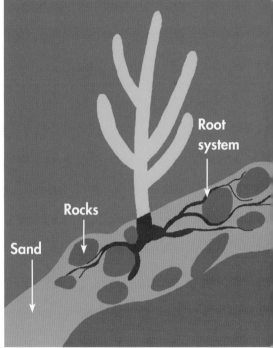

Root system

Rocks

Sand

Cactus plants have thick **stems**. When it rains, the stems collect and store water for the plants to use later.

Cactus plants have long **roots** that grow close to the surface of the ground. These roots help the plants absorb as much water as possible after it rains.

Find out more

Which is the largest cactus that grows in the world? How tall can it grow?

Plant roots travel deep into cracks in the rock.

Some plants can grow in rocky places.

Growing in rocky cracks

Some plants can grow in rocky places where there is very little soil.

The wind blows small amounts of **soil** into cracks in the rock. When rain runs into the cracks, the plants use this soil and water to grow. Their roots creep along and down the cracks.

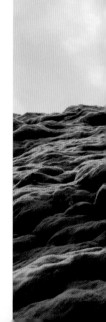

Did you know?

Moss can grow on bare rocks.

9

Chapter 2

How do plants grow in very cold places?

Some plants can grow in very cold places where the ground is frozen for most of the year. These plants rest for nine months under the snow while it is very cold.

Some plants can grow in very cold places.

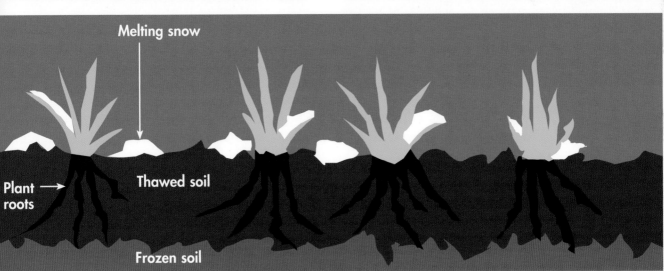

Melting snow

Plant roots →

Thawed soil

Frozen soil

In summer, the snow **melts**, and the top of the frozen ground starts to **thaw**. The **roots** of the plants grow down as far as they can in the ground.

Melting snow makes pools of water on the ground. Some plants use this water to grow, and they get food from small amounts of **soil** in the water.

Growing on high mountains

Some plants **cling** to and spread across the sides of rocks and mountains. The leaves of these plants collect energy from the sun and change it into food.

The plants grow in small groups low on the ground. This helps to protect them from the wind and the cold. The sunlight can spread over the whole low plant more quickly to give it energy as it grows. The plants have small leaves that keep in any water.

On high mountains, plants grow low on the ground.

13

Chapter 3

How do plants grow in and near the sea?

Growing in salty water

Salt kills most plants, but some plants can grow in salty water. These plants grow in **shallow**, salty water near the edge of the sea where the sunlight is able to get through to them. They use the energy from the sunlight to help them grow.

Mangrove plants grow in salty water.

Mangrove plants grow near the edge of the sea. They have roots that are like **filters**. The roots keep out some of the salt in the seawater.

Some salt is stored in the leaves of the mangrove plant. The plant gets rid of the salt by dropping its leaves.

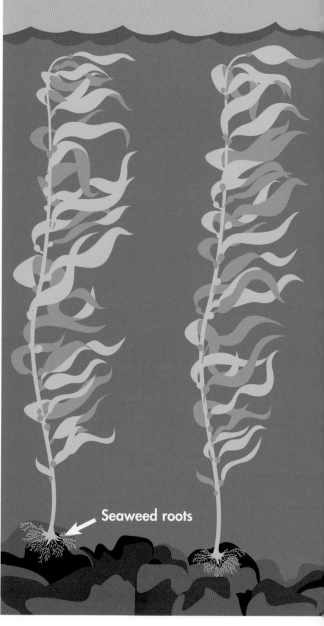

Seaweed roots

Find out more

What other plants grow in shallow, salty water?

Seaweed grows on rocks or in sand under salty water. Its roots **cling** to these places so that the waves do not wash the plant away. Seaweed does not need fresh water to survive.

16

Some plants can grow in sand.

Growing in sand or mud

The rounded noon flower can grow in sand or mud near the sea. It stores rainwater in its thick leaves and uses it to grow.

Conclusion

Plants can grow almost anywhere in the world. Some
plants have ways of surviving even in hot, dry, and
rocky places, very cold places, and in places where
there is a lot of salt. They are still able to get the
things they need to grow in these **harsh** places.

Glossary

cling to stick to something as if glued to it

filters structures that stop too much salt water from entering a plant

harsh unpleasant and difficult

mangrove a plant that can live partly in salty water

melts when a substance changes from a solid to a liquid, usually when it is heated

roots the parts of a plant that grow under the ground

shallow being close to the surface

soil the top layer of the land, often called dirt

stems the long, thin parts of plants that support the leaves and flowers

thaw to stop being frozen

Index